Walks on the
Northumberland
Coast

David Haffey

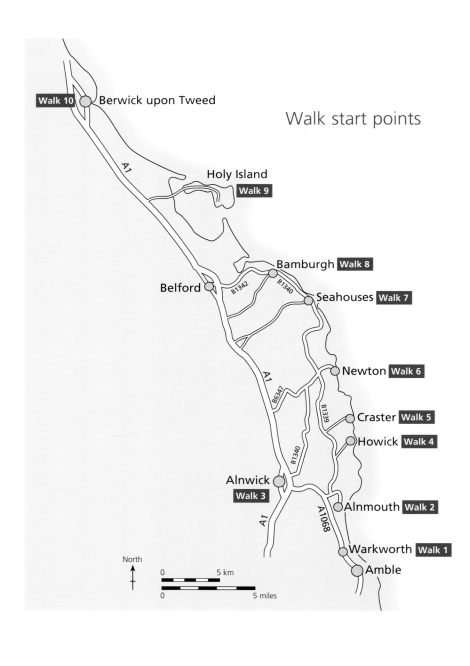

Walk start points

Walk 10 — Berwick upon Tweed

Holy Island
Walk 9

Bamburgh — Walk 8

Belford

B1342

B1340

Seahouses — Walk 7

A1

B6347

Newton — Walk 6

B1339

Craster — Walk 5

Howick — Walk 4

B1340

Alnwick
Walk 3

A1

A1068

Alnmouth — Walk 2

Warkworth — Walk 1

Amble

North

0   5 km

0   5 miles

Contents

Introduction

This book describes a number of routes allowing both visitors and local people to experience and enjoy the north Northumberland coast. The routes vary in length from about 2½ to 5½ miles and most can be completed in half a day or less, even by relatively inexperienced walkers. Generally the routes are level or have very modest hill-climbs but remember that walking along sandy beaches can be tiring.

The North Northumberland Coast is an Area of Outstanding Natural Beauty, rich in scenery, wildlife and history and retaining a sense of peace and tranquillity.

For centuries this part of Northumbria occupied a strategic position, as a gateway to settlement and conquest for Angles and Danes, kings and peasant-farmers. It became part of the troubled borderland between England and Scotland, then a battle-hardened stronghold in the Wars of the Roses. The coastal cliffs of the Whin Sill were irresistible for anyone needing a castle. Some of these fortifications are now romantic ruins, but others have been carefully preserved. Many of the walks described in this book pass close by the most imposing castles and provide an opportunity to discover more about their history.

Northumberland had a peaceful side to its past too. During the 7th and 8th centuries the monastery on Lindisfarne, or Holy Island as it often now called, was a centre for Christian learning, craft and culture. The Lindisfarne Gospels remain one of the world's outstanding early Christian achievements.

These walks also provide an opportunity to appreciate the wildlife of the Northumberland coast. In spring and early summer, the dunes and coastal grasslands are covered with wildflowers: cowslips, primroses and a host of herbs and blossoms lost to most of the countryside are still abundant here. Spring is also a good time to see grey seals which, on calm days, like to laze on offshore rocks, watching people from a safe distance. The seals breed on the Farne Islands in early winter; these waters are considered to be among the finest marine habitats in Europe, attracting anything from lumpsuckers and jellyfish to passing dolphins and whales.

In autumn and winter the coast is home to many thousands of wildfowl and waders. Lindisfarne is a National Nature Reserve and is famous for arctic migrants, such as warblers, flycatchers and chats, and for its flocks of wintering pale-bellied brent geese. In spring and summer the islands are alive with nesting sea-birds; it is a common sight to see puffins returning from fishing trips, eiders shepherding rafts of ducklings, and terns being chased by piratical skuas. On a coast walk you are almost certain to see something wonderful.

Maps and Rights of Way

The majority of the walks follow public footpaths and bridleways; together they form part of the public rights of way network maintained by Northumberland County Council. These are usually signposted only where they leave a metalled road. Elsewhere, alternative routes have been used where these have been provided by a local landowner, or are used with their consent: in these cases the routes are marked as permissive paths. The walks sometimes make use of the shoreline, the intertidal area for which no defined rights of way exist but open access is usually allowed. Where there is no suitable alternative, the walks follow public roads but, for safety reasons, these lengths have been kept to a minimum: where possible, walkers should always use the pavement or verge and keep a careful watch for oncoming vehicles.

The route symbols used on the maps are as follows:

———— Public right of way

······· Permissive path

At the start of each walk there is a brief introduction to describe the walk and to give an indication of its length and the route that it follows. Interpretive notes describing points of interest along the way are printed in blue type, whilst route directions are given in black type. Where necessary, the Ordnance Survey grid reference is given for the start of the walk: details of how to use this are printed on the 1: 50000 Landranger series. All of the walks in this book are covered by OS Explorer Maps (1:25,000) Nos. 332, 340 & 346 and by OS Landranger Maps (1:50,000) Nos. 75 & 81.

Along many of the walks you will see finger posts and waymarkers for the Northumberland Coast Path, a 103 kilometre (64 mile) walking route that forms part of a pan-European 'North Sea Trial'. From Cresswell (near Ashington) the Coast Path hugs the coast as far as Bamburgh before heading inland to Belford and the Kyloe Hills. From here it joins St. Cuthbert's Way and returns to the coast at Holy Island before continuing to Berwick-upon-Tweed. For further information on these routes see **www.northumberlandcoastaonb.org** and **www.ldwa.org.uk**

Enjoy your Walk

Comfort is essential to the enjoyment of any walk so wear sensible shoes or boots: ideally these should be lightweight and waterproof. Remember also that rocky shores can be slippy and uneven: it is therefore advisable to use footwear that supports the ankle and has a non-slip sole.

Walking may seem to be warm work but sea breezes can often be deceptively cool and it is best to take a sweater or fleece: a lightweight waterproof will also keep out the wind as well as the rain.

Safety Advice

All but one of these walks are on the coast and there are a number of points that should be borne in mind, especially if you are taking young children.

Tides and Rivers
If the sea is rough or the tide is high, keep well above the shoreline, especially on rocky areas where sea spray can make the ground slippy or large breakers might catch you unawares. In several places the text gives an alternative route if you are unsure. When the tide is out, watch for areas of soft sand and always be alert to the possibility of being cut off by an incoming tide. Some of the walks also run alongside rivers: be careful with young children and don't be tempted to paddle or swim - the water can be deceptively deep and cold, even at the height of summer.

Weather
Weather can change very rapidly on the coast. Bright sunshine can be quickly obscured by fog and mist rolling in off the sea - this can sometimes spread well inland. If this looks likely to happen, think twice about setting out or take extra care and warm, waterproof clothing.

Cliffs
In one or two places the routes follow cliff tops: on these sections don't go near the edge and take special care if you have young children or dogs with you.

Golf Courses
Good stretches of coast are ideal for golf courses and there are several in this part of Northumberland. Two of the walks cross or go alongside golf courses and a number of others pass close by. Remember that even the most experienced golfer has wayward shots, so keep a weather eye for such mishaps and always give way to golfers who may be hitting a ball in your direction.

Looking after the Countryside

Most of the land along these walks is privately owned. It is in everyone's interest to look after the countryside and to leave it as we would like to find it. In particular, fasten all gates and keep to the recognised route, especially when crossing farmland. It is also important to act responsibly and considerately by keeping to the Country Code; take any litter home and, if you wish to take a dog, keep it under control, preferably on a lead. The Northumberland coast is important for a wide variety of wildlife, with several areas being designated as Sites of Special Scientific Interest: visitors should take care to safeguard this valuable part of our natural heritage by avoiding disturbance to plants and animals and their habitats.

1. Warkworth, Church Hill and the Aln

BESIDE DUNE, SHORE AND ESTUARY for a distance of 5½ miles, starting close to a mediaeval town and making for the site of a Saxon church on a grassy rivermouth knoll. Good views of Coquet Island and Alnmouth, and a fine stretch of golden sand on the way back. An easy walk with very little climbing, except for the few metres to reach the top of historic Church Hill, from where the best views of the estuary and coast can be gained.

Park in the Northumberland County Council car park at Warkworth Dunes Picnic Site, at grid reference NU 255064. This is reached along the small side-road (signed to the Beach and Warkworth Golf Club) that branches off the A1068, immediately to the north of the bridge over the River Coquet on the northern edge of Warkworth village.

Take the stony path from the car park down towards the sea, past the golf course, and then through the dunes to the beach. Turn left and head north along the shoreline.

The dunes are being eaten away by high tides and winter gales. On this part of the coast the longshore drift is north to south: the sand eroded from these dunes is being carried by the tides and is clogging up the entrance to Amble harbour about a mile to the south.

The beach is often flecked with black shiny pebbles. This is sea-coal, washed up from seams outcropping on the sea bed. In times of hardship, local people were happy to gather the black bounty; it burnt badly, but it was free.

After about half a mile, as the beach starts to take a gentle curve to the right, turn left through a cut in the dunes and follow the grass path under a high wooden footbridge. Continue across the golf course (watching out for golfers coming from the right) and, on the far side, turn right along a stone track and through a gate.

Warkworth Castle

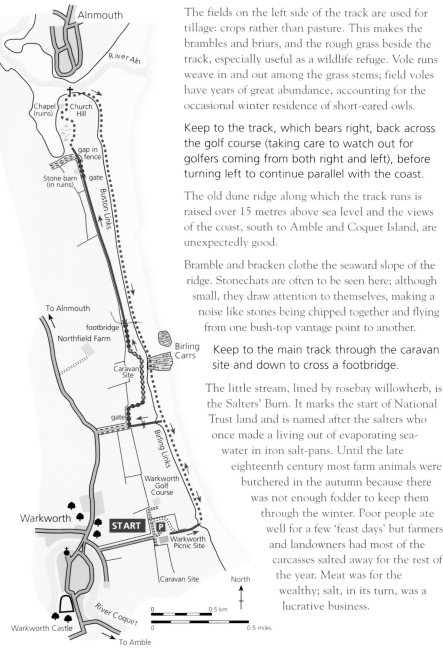

The fields on the left side of the track are used for tillage: crops rather than pasture. This makes the brambles and briars, and the rough grass beside the track, especially useful as a wildlife refuge. Vole runs weave in and out among the grass stems; field voles have years of great abundance, accounting for the occasional winter residence of short-eared owls.

Keep to the track, which bears right, back across the golf course (taking care to watch out for golfers coming from both right and left), before turning left to continue parallel with the coast.

The old dune ridge along which the track runs is raised over 15 metres above sea level and the views of the coast, south to Amble and Coquet Island, are unexpectedly good.

Bramble and bracken clothe the seaward slope of the ridge. Stonechats are often to be seen here; although small, they draw attention to themselves, making a noise like stones being chipped together and flying from one bush-top vantage point to another.

Keep to the main track through the caravan site and down to cross a footbridge.

The little stream, lined by rosebay willowherb, is the Salters' Burn. It marks the start of National Trust land and is named after the salters who once made a living out of evaporating sea-water in iron salt-pans. Until the late eighteenth century most farm animals were butchered in the autumn because there was not enough fodder to keep them through the winter. Poor people ate well for a few 'feast days' but farmers and landowners had most of the carcasses salted away for the rest of the year. Meat was for the wealthy; salt, in its turn, was a lucrative business.

9

The low bushes growing to the right of the path after the burn are blackthorns. Gnarled and pruned by the wind and impossibly dense, this bed of thorns still brings out a show of white flowers in April and enjoys a few days of fragile beauty. The sloe berries later in the year seem a more appropriate gift from the east wind: bitter as gall.

Follow the footpath up an old dune ridge then down again, following a wall on the left.

The heathland and marshy ground in the hollow to the left lies at the head of a southern spur of the Aln estuary. Mudflats may once have extended further up the hollow but the sea currents changed and on Christmas Day in 1806 there was a fierce storm. This finally caused the river to change course, sending it north of Church Hill, and the basin behind the ridge of Buston Links may have silted up as a consequence. What had been saltings was reclaimed, but not to anything more than rough pasture. The sweep of open country is a winter hunting ground for merlins and hen harriers. Pipits and starlings are their main prey.

Continue along the path, with the spire of Alnmouth Church in the distance ahead, and past a ruined stone barn in the field to the left.

In the 19th century, when the river passed close by, the barn was used as a store for guano imported on schooners from South America. It is not surprising that this building was kept well away for the town because guano, which in those days was an important agricultural fertiliser, is formed from seabird and bat droppings and is extremely smelly.

About 100 metres past the ruined barn, as the stone track turns to the left (signed to 'Hipsburn' and the 'Coast Path'), keep straight ahead to go through a gap in a fence. Follow the grass path through the dunes, then bear right around the edge of the mudflats and make for the mound of Church Hill.

The ruined chapel on Church Hill

North west over the Aln Estuary from the top of Church Hill

Saltings and mudflats have their own kind of beauty, appreciated by birds rather than by people. The grey ooze, covered by a sparse carpet of sea purslane, is rich in worms and crustacea; the redshank ('warden of the marshes'), is a constant feature but this is also the place for curlew and grey plover. Most waders have far-carrying calls, the essence of wide open places.

Go past the ruin of a small chapel and climb to the top of Church Hill.

The first real historian in Britain was the Venerable Bede of St Paul's Monastery in Jarrow. His hero was St. Cuthbert, the greatest of all the northern saints, who was created bishop of Lindisfarne at a synod in 684. According to Bede, the synod or meeting took place at 'Aettwifordia', translated as Twiford or the place of two fords.

Church Hill was much bigger before the river changed course. There had been a broad platform on which had stood a Norman Church dedicated to St. John the Baptist which had, in turn, been built over the site of a Saxon Church dedicated to St. Waleric. Bede's description, and the circumstantial evidence, point to this being the place of the famous synod. But with most of it washed away, nobody is ever going to be sure.

The chapel or oratory, which makes a pretty ruin and has a very obvious Norman arch over the door, was built in 1869. Nearby are concrete slabs from the sexton's house, built at the same time. Church Hill is a curious and enigmatic place.

Alnmouth and its harbour are set out below, a colourful and busy place even though its days as a commercial port ended more than a century ago. It made its money by exporting grain. In return it imported anything from timber to guano: there was a sawmill close to Waterside House, to the west across the saltings, and guano sheds to the south (of which only the one remains), well downwind of the town.

Waterside House Farm figures in one of Alnmouth's most colourful little adventures. In the early evening of 23 September 1779, shortly after the American War of Independence and when Britain was still at war with France, the pirate John Paul Jones appeared off the coast in his ship Ranger. After cruising up and down for a while he attacked a brig, then sailed south firing a parting cannon-shot at the substantial ruins of St Waleric's. The shot missed, but the 28 lb. cannonball demolished the gable-end of Waterside House. This was bad luck on the farmer, and a bad shot by Jones, but why he chose to fire at all is a mystery. Cannonballs weren't cheap.

From Church Hill follow a path north to the end of the dune ridge and, taking care on the steep descent, continue down onto the beach. Turn right and walk along the high tide line. If the tide is high - especially at Birling Carrs where the sea can reach the base of the cliffs - climb up onto the dunes to follow the path taken on the outward leg of the walk or pick your own path along the dune ridge.

From this perspective the dunes don't look quite so stable; there are several places where the wind has found a loophole and taken a bite out of the ridge. The process of erosion and deposition is going on all the time; the wartime concrete blocks (anti-tank defences) look vulnerable against such elemental force.

Coquet Island lies about four miles away to the south-east, off Hauxley Point and Amble harbour. The tranquil view belies the reality of Coquet Island; several ships have come to grief on the adjacent rocks. The lighthouse stands on the site of a Benedictine monastery, which is where Elfleda (Abbess of Whitby and sister of King Ecgfrith of Northumbria) had a meeting with Cuthbert in 684 to convince him he should take on the bishopric of Hexham. He did, but was never happy in the task and soon gave it up in favour of his beloved Lindisfarne.

Apart from a brief notoriety in the Civil War, nothing else has happened on Coquet Island. It is an RSPB reserve and is significant for its colonies of roseate terns and eider ducks (this is as far south as they nest).

Continue past the rock shelf at Birling Carrs and the gap in the dunes with the high timber footbridge featured early in the walk. Follow the shoreline for another half mile. At the next gap, broad with low dunes, take the path next to a lifebelt and along the stone track beside the golf course, back to the car park.

Warkworth is a charming and historic village, well worth exploring. From the Warkworth Dunes Car Park it is a walk of slightly more than half a mile each way. Alternatively, take the car and park in the town centre, close to the old market cross and the church of St Lawrence.

There is a great deal to Warkworth; it is one of the most perfect mediaeval towns in the north of England and has all the key ingredients associated with a hilltop site on a river-loop. The castle is situated at the top of the main street (Castle Street) and is open to the public: it has been in a ruinous state since Tudor times but its stonework looks good for another thousand years. At close quarters the very stones seem to breathe history. Crucifixes scratched into dark corners of dungeon cells hint at cruel justice and desperate souls.

The rest of Warkworth lies in the castle's ample shadow and is not to the same grand scale, which has helped to preserve its character. The market cross is plain and enigmatic; the church is Norman but has some Saxon stonework and a cross dating back to the days of King Ceolwulf.

Alongside the modern road bridge over the River Coquet is a much older two-arched stone bridge. The road north out of the town must have been no more than a narrow track even in its heyday. The little bridge, hump-backed and cobbled, was built in 1379 to replace an older structure, and the stone tower on the town side was added to allow the gate to be closed to unwelcome visitors . The castle made Warkworth a strategic target. The fortified bridge was intended to prevent the kind of attack that had taken place in 1174 when William the Lion's army had put a torch to the town and slaughtered over a hundred people who had been hiding in the church. Life was cheap; what looks quaint and modest now was a mediaeval version of civil defence and home insurance.

Warkworth Castle and the River Coquet

2. Alnmouth, Lesbury & Foxton Hall

A GENTLE WALK BESIDE THE RIVER ALN. About 4 miles long, following the river as it wanders through flat fields and saltmarshes before squeezing between grassy knolls at its outfall. Estuaries are few and far between in the north-east and this one has the added advantage of being compact and pretty. Historic settlements, pirates, cuddy ducks and a fine sweep of sand complete the picture.

Park in the car park beside the beach at Alnmouth Common. This is reached by turning right at the small roundabout on entering the town then, after 50 metres, turn left along 'The Wynd', following the sign to the car & coach park. Over the brow of the hill, bear left across the golf course and park in the car park to the right of the old lifeboat station.

From the car park, cross the grass bank onto the beach. Turn right and walk along the upper beach towards the mouth of the River Aln.

Alnmouth beach was at its most fashionable in Victorian times; it was Prince Albert who started the British obsession with the seaside, and for affluent Tynesiders this was the ideal spot. They arrived by train, at Bilton Junction, and were then driven to the stylish hotels (Hope and Anchor, Schooner and Red Lion), from where they promenaded, breathed the bracing air, and took tea. Whilst all this was going on, there was another side to the town. In 1895 there had been a famous riot, caused by the 'excessive thirst' of a gang of Amble fishermen. The Alnmouth policeman arrested one of the drunks, whereupon the rioters stormed (or staggered) about the town. All they actually did was to abuse a methodist minister and kill the policeman's canary (by accident). Justice dictated that they were all sent to gaol for up to two years.

Alnmouth Harbour from Church Hill

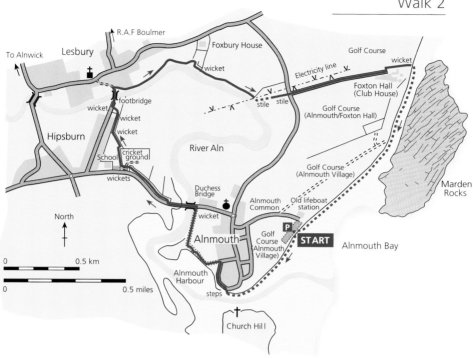

Out to sea lies Coquet Island, an important breeding site for the rarest and most elegant of the terns, the roseate, and the most southerly nesting site for the eider duck.

Turn right into the mouth of the estuary, opposite a large grassy mound on the far bank.

The mound is Church Hill, on which once stood the ruins of the Norman church of St John the Baptist (see Walk 1).

Where the dunes meet the harbour wall, climb the stone steps on the right and turn left along the road in front of the houses.

Alnmouth grew up as a port, its face turned to the sea, and there is a hint of self confidence in its buildings. The town reached its heyday in the 18th century, exporting wheat (carted in from Hexham along the turnpike road) and importing Scandinavian raw materials such as timber. There was also a local fishing industry and a boat building business; this sheltered mooring must have been a busy place and it is still used by small yachts and dinghies.

Walk past a childrens' playground on the left. As the road turns right up Garden Terrace, go sharp left along Lovers Walk, a narrow path tucked between the electricity sub-station and an old wooden barn.

Estuaries are rare on the north-east coast; usually the rivers are short, straight, and are flowing too fast to deposit very much sediment. The Aln is different, and below Lesbury it meanders across a broad valley, which slows it down and lets it unload mud and silt as it turns towards the sea. Eel grass, sea purslane and sea aster cover the slake or salting, and beside the path in the summer there are patches of ragwort and scurvy-grass. Intertidal mud, the glistening grey ooze along the hidden creeks, is rich in nutrients and is full of worms and shellfish; these in turn feed shelduck and waders such as godwits and curlews.

The path leads to Duchess Bridge. Go up the steps and through a wicket-gate. Taking care to watch for traffic, cross the road and go around the end of the stone parapet to cross the river via a metal footway attached to the bridge.

The bridge was built in 1864 to link the town with the nearest railway station. The river is tidal, and both right and left of the bridge there are levees or embankments to keep floodwater off the surrounding fields.

About 100 metres beyond the bridge, bear right onto a gravel path on the far side of the roadside hedge. Go through a wicket gate at the end of the path and across the access track to the cricket ground. A few metres further on, go through another wicket gate and turn sharp right along a grass path beside a hedge.

Just past the corner of the cricket ground, the path dog-legs to the right of a line of old hawthorn trees. Go through a wicket gate, with gardens to the left and the field fence on your right. About 50 metres past a wicket gate at the end of the houses, the path bears left and leads through a wicket gate onto a road. Turn right along the road and onto the footbridge over the River Aln.

The footbridge over the River Aln at Lesbury

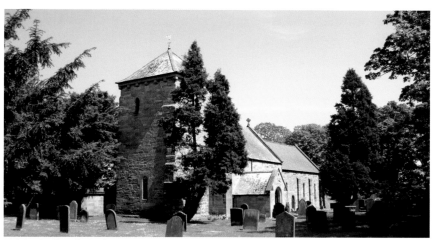

St Mary's Church, Lesbury

Hard to believe this is the same river! Instead of tide-swept purslane, the banks are covered with herbs and shrubs. During the summer there are huge clumps of butterbur, like giant rhubarb. The leaves were used to wrap butter and cheese, hence the name.

At the end of the bridge railings, cut back sharp right (signed to 'Alnmouth' and 'Foxton Hall') across a patch of grass to a small wooden footbridge and follow the riverside path heading downstream. If you have time, it is worth taking a short detour into Lesbury: instead of turning right at the end of the railings, continue along the narrow path between the cottages up to the road. The church is straight ahead and the centre of the village (with Post Office and pub) is to the left.

Once upon a time Lesbury was as big as Alnwick and more important than Alnmouth. But instead of the cut and thrust of commerce, Lesbury served a farming community and owed its dues to the Duke of Northumberland. Whilst other towns flourished, Lesbury drifted along in its own quiet way. St Mary's Church was supported by Alnwick Abbey and then by the Duke, which explains its relative size. For many years it also had to be used by the people of Alnmouth, who were obliged to pay twice as much for weddings and funerals as the local community. The relationship between the two communities has always been delicate.

Henry, the 7th Duke of Northumberland, is buried in Lesbury churchyard along with his family. According to inscriptions on the gravestones they are all 'sleeping' except for the Duke's son, Earl Henry Algernon, who is said to have been shot in a duel and is therefore listed as having died.

If you took the detour into Lesbury, retrace your steps to the footbridge and follow the riverside path heading downstream (signed to 'Alnmouth' and 'Foxton Hall').

The lower reaches of the River Aln looking towards Hipsburn and Lesbury

Until a few years ago the large field to your left was a pasture that hadn't been ploughed for decades, if not centuries. Its surface was then still corrugated with the ridge and furrow lines created when ploughs were pulled by teams of oxen. Because these ploughs couldn't be reversed when the team was turned around at the end of a run, the cumulative effect, as years went by, was to throw the earth into low parallel ridges: this had the beneficial effect of improving drainage. Modern ploughing destroys these historic cultivation patterns and sadly they are no longer visible in this field.

Below Foxbury House, keep to the path that cuts to the right through the gorse and back down to the river bank to go through a wicket gate.

Back to the tidal river again! Most freshwater plants find it hard to live with salt water, but common reed copes quite well. Its bleached stems and flower-heads last through the winter and provide cover for reed buntings and water rails. Extensive beds of reeds are rare in the north of England, but at East Chevington, close to Druridge Bay, a 100 acre reed-bed has been created on a restored opencast coal site in the hope of attracting bearded tit, marsh harrier and bittern. At present, the nearest breeding site for these dwindling species is at Leighton Moss in Lancashire.

At the stile next to the electricity pole turn left, keeping the line of poles slightly to your left as you climb the steep (but short) hillside.

A seat at the top of the hill offers the chance of a welcome rest and time to enjoy the view back over the Aln valley and across to Alnwick Moor. The outline of the Cheviot massif is just visible in the far distance over the red roofs of the houses in Hipsburn village.

Continue over a stile and onto a road. Cross the road and go down the drive signed to 'Alnmouth Golf Club - Foxton Hall'.

Foxton has always prided itself on being a distinct, well-healed community. The Hall is part of the Ducal estate and has been a golf club since 1930. Norway spruce trees do their best to shade the approach to the club-house but they are not suited to a mild maritime climate - they come from Scandinavia and central Europe and prefer long hard winters with sub zero temperatures.

At the Club House, go past the Visitors' Car Park and take the path to the left of the Members' Car Park sign. This path bears right down a concrete track towards the sea. Go through the wicket gate and turn right along the beach.

If the tide is in there is an alternative inland route back to Alnmouth. About 200 metres south of the wicket gate onto the beach, and just to the right of a low stone breakwater, climb the steep path up the bank and follow this along the edge of Foxton Golf Course. This gradually takes you further inland along a ridge above Alnmouth Village Golf Course but it is well signed and eventually brings you to the access road between the village and the car park.

The sweep of Alnmouth Bay lies ahead. It can be a glorious sight, but it can also be cold and windswept. The wooden groynes are intended to stop the sand from being blown away. Further along, at the top of the beach, are a row of concrete blocks that were built to slow Hitler's invasion. No tanks ever landed, so perhaps the idea worked.

John Paul Jones was not the only pirate to plough the waves of Alnmouth Bay (see Walk 1). There were at least four other attacks on local shipping in the mid 18th century, usually by French privateers. The German Ocean, as the North Sea was then called, was a dangerous place.

Continue along the tideline, back to the car park beyond the old lifeboat station.

Alnmouth Village from the ridge path above the golf course

3. Alnwick Castle

IN MEDIAEVAL TIMES castles were built to impress, to inspire fear in enemies and loyalty in friends. They are still a powerful theme in the countryside. Wherever you walk around the ancient town of Alnwick the castle is towering over your shoulder. Down the river, in a beautiful setting of parkland, woodland and pastures, it is possible to step back and see the feudal fortress in its context, at the heart of a great estate.

At a time when landscape conservation is a luxury we can hardly afford, this gentle walk of just under four miles lets you catch your breath and share a vision of Albion.

Park in the town centre car park on Greenwell Road, signed off the main road close to the Hotspur Tower on the southern side of the town.

Walk back up Greenwell Road and turn left along the main road past the Alnwick Playhouse.

Alnwick's walls disappeared centuries ago, but its main gate survives. When it was built in 1452, this tower was intended to intimidate and impress, and some of its hidden chambers were used as prison cells. These days the tower serves to define the town's place in history, to whet the appetite of visitors. 'Hotspur' was the nickname of Henry Percy, the swashbuckling son of the first Earl of Northumberland. He was killed fighting against the king at the battle of Shrewsbury; the tower was built about forty years later by his son, the second earl. Above the gateway, which acts as a bottleneck for anyone driving into town, is a sandstone panel on which the weathered outline of the Brabant lion, emblem of the Percy family, is just visible.

At the war memorial, turn left down the hill along Denwick Lane (the B1340 signed to Bamburgh and Denwick).

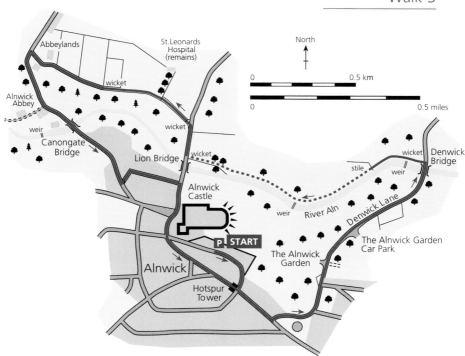

The Percy lion, with its curious ramrod tail, makes a dramatic appearance on the top of a doric column, visible through the trees on the right. The proper name of this monument is the Percy Tenantry Column, built in 1816 by the Duke's grateful tenants after he had reduced their rents during the lean times of the Napoleonic Wars. The column's nickname was the Farmers' Folly.

Continue down Denwick Lane past the entrance to The Alnwick Garden.

The Alnwick Garden opened in 2002 and is widely regarded as one of the most exciting contemporary gardens to be developed in the UK over the last century. It was the brainchild of the Duchess of Northumberland and is proving to be an extremely popular tourist attraction - being seen by some as the 'Eden Project of the North'. It is certainly worth a visit and includes something for all the family, with spectacular water fountains and cascades, beautiful gardens (including a Rose Garden, Poison Garden and Ornamental Garden), a Pavilion and Visitor Centre, and one of the largest tree houses in the world.

Past the Garden entrance, and over the wall on the left, is a beech plantation. The Percy family once owned more land than anyone in England and the estate is still vast. Most of it is farmland leased to tenants, but some is managed directly by the Northumberland Estates. This plantation is a good example of woodland that is both attractive and valuable. The best trees for timber are tall and straight, without side-

Alnwick Castle

branches or knots, and this is why these beech are grown close together. The wood is used for furniture and veneers, but the investment is long-term - at least 80 to 100 years.

At Denwick Bridge the road crosses the River Aln and you get your first view of Alnwick Castle, perfectly proportioned and in an ideal setting of parkland and water. The bridge was built by John Adam for the first Duke of Northumberland in the late 18th century. The balustrade on the left takes the form of linked half moons, the emblem of the Northumberland Estates.

Immediately after Denwick Bridge, turn sharp left through a wicket gate (signed 'Public Footpath – Lion Bridge') and walk along the grassy path, keeping the river to the left. After about 300 metres, cross the stile. At this point the public right of way strikes off to the right along the fence line but, by kind permission of His Grace the Duke of Northumberland, visitors are allowed to use the riverside path.

The river is deliberately pretty; weirs have been built to back up the current and create wide dark pools. In summer the banks are lined with flowers: meadowsweet, water avens, brooklime and marsh marigold.

Alnwick Castle owes its present mediaeval splendour to restoration work of the 18th and 19th centuries. In fact, the original fortress was built in Norman times, knocked down bit by bit, redesigned and enlarged and finally left derelict by the turn of the 17th century. The rebuild of the 1850s was to transmute a Gothic monster created in the 1760s; it cost a quarter of a million pounds to put things right and add a few flourishes such as the Prudhoe Tower. The result, as seen reflected in the Aln, is a castle of dreams, the 'Windsor of the North'.

Continue along the riverside path, making for the Lion Bridge.

The sweep of pasture is called the Park. The panorama from the river bend is as classic a view as you could wish to see anywhere. At first glance there is nothing contemporary in the landscape; no pylons, no telegraph poles and no houses. However, the wire fences, large fields and distant crops (winter barley, oilseed rape) are a giveaway. To the right on the far skyline is a line of trees marking a battlefield; it was here that Malcolm, King of Scotland was mortally wounded in 1093 whilst laying siege to the castle (it was then a motte and bailey). In 1174 another Scottish king, William the Lion, also had cause to rue his attack on Alnwick. He was captured but lived on to be an threat to King John.

Before the bridge there is a very nice piece of wetland off to the left along the riverbank. Where the river widens there are beds of reed, providing cover for nesting moorhens, mallard and dabchick. Otters live on the Aln too, though they are strictly nocturnal and rarely seen.

At the end of the riverside path, go through a wicket gate and cross the road (TAKE CARE!) onto a pavement. The route of the walk turns right up the hill, but before doing so, have a look at the Lion Bridge a few metres to the left.

Another classic view of the Aln. The bridge, complete with lead lion, dates back to 1773. It replaced a narrow mediaeval structure damaged in a flood in 1770.

Retrace your steps and walk up the hill. About 200 metres from the bridge, as the road starts to bend right, turn left through a gap in the wall to a wicket gate. Through the wicket gate, continue along the grass path with a wall to the left and fields to the right.

The Lion Bridge from the riverside path

The woodland on the left is a rich wildlife habitat, very mixed and with glades and thickets. Migrant songbirds such as blackcaps and redstarts nest here, and on mild summer evenings you can often see noctule bats and woodcock.

To the right is Radcliffe's Close, an area of land once owned by the ill-fated Earls of Derwentwater. At the end of a row of trees (to the right of the first gate) are the remains of St. Leonard's Hospital, founded at the turn of the 13th century. Nearby is a well where Malcolm was brought after the battle of 1093. He died here and Eustace de Vescey, the Norman Lord of Alnwick, had the hospital built in his memory.

After passing through an unfenced section of pasture, go through a wicket gate to continue along the wall-side path. This leads to the little hamlet of Abbeylands: here, walk along the driveway straight ahead to join a road, then turn left down the hill, keeping to the roadside pavement.

In the wall-end on the left there is an unusual little letter box, with the inscription of Edward VII. He only reigned for nine years between 1902 and 1910, so letter boxes from this period are quite rare - unlike those dating from the reign of his predecessor, Queen Victoria.

On the right as you walk down the road is Hulne Park and the gatehouse of Alnwick Abbey. The abbey was founded for a colony of White Canons in 1147 and had an uneventful history, which probably suited them nicely in such troubled times. In 1304, one of the priors wrote a poem (in latin) about a shady character called Robin Hood. Whether the story was fiction or fact no-one will ever know. The abbey disappeared with the Dissolution in 1549; apart from the gatehouse, which looks as if it has floated away from the nearby castle, nothing remains.

Cross Canongate Bridge and continue into the town.

This is the third bridge over the Aln, built in 1821 and without any decoration. Like the others, it replaced a much older structure, a wooden footbridge.

Continue right, up the hill along Canongate. Just before the church, turn sharp left down a side road: this heads downhill for a short distance and then bears right. Keep to the pavement on the left side of the road.

Set into the weathered sandstone wall on the left is a mullioned window and an arched doorway. This was the entrance to the Chantry ('St Mary's Chauntry-house'), founded in 1449 and used by the chaplains of St Mary's and St Michael's as a school for 'poor boys in the art of Grammar gratis'.

At the T junction, cross the road and turn right up the hill along The Peth towards the town centre. At the top of the hill the road leads right, past the entrance to the Alnwick Castle, then left around the castle walls.

The castle is open from April to October and it is hard to resist its lure. History is etched into every stone, and each stone tells a different story.

Continue along Bailiffgate and Narrowgate past the Oddfellows Arms.

Opposite Pottergate and its pant (or circular trough) is an inn called Ye Olde Cross, more commonly known as the Dirty Bottles. In the window stands a row of dusty bottles over 150 years old. According to local legend, a man collapsed and died whilst moving them; no-one has dared finish the job and the bottles have remained half-cleared.

The road bears left to Bondgate, the main street through Alnwick. Continue past Hotspur Tower and turn left, back along Greenwell Road to the car park.

The Gatehouse – all that remains of Alnwick Abbey

4. Howick & Craster

ALONG THE COAST PATH and above a dramatic rocky shore to the fishing village of Craster, then back across rolling farmland towards Howick Hall. Craster makes a perfect half-way point with all necessary facilities, including a restaurant that specialises in its own famous kippers. Easy walking of about 4½ miles.

Park at grid reference NU 259174, on the broad side-road verge just off the Howick-Craster road, before Sea Houses Farm.

Over the field inland to the west is a line of woodland following the Howick Burn to its outfall half a mile to the south at Iron Scars. Cushat Wood and Crow Wood join with other sections of oak/elm woodland to make an attractive patchwork of tree-lines. 'Cushat' is the local name for the wood pigeon, 'crow' probably refers to rooks rather than carrion crows, which are known in Northumberland as corbies.

Walk the few metres back along the side-road to where it meets the main road, then turn right through a wicket-gate and along a track towards the sea. Go through the wicket-gate at the end of the track and bear left (north), past a house perched above the shore.

If you take a short detour to the right after passing through the gate at the end of the track, this will take you along a grass path that leads down to a lovely little sandy bay. The sandstone cliffs offer some shelter from sea breezes, making it a great place for a picnic or a bar-b-cue and, once you have finished the walk, you could come back and even have a paddle to refresh your tired feet.

The Victorian bathing house near Howick

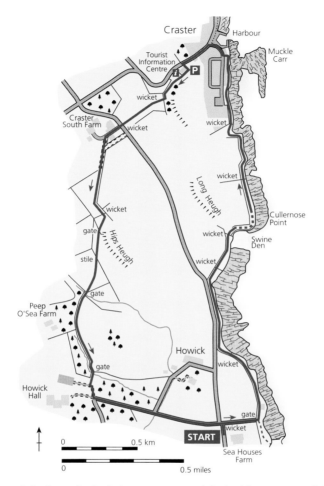

The sandstone cliffs above the little bay were quarried for building stone and the faces are heavily weathered. The cross-bedding of the sandstone, created when the rock was laid down by cross-currents of estuary tides, has been sculpted away at different rates by the wind leaving some beautiful bas-relief patterns.

The small house on the cliff top is a 19th century bathing house built by the Grey family who lived at nearby Howick Hall. The ornate chimney pots make a great finishing touch and are the type architectural detail so loved by the Victorians. The Grey's would have taken picnics with them and spread these outside if the weather was fine: if not, they had a fire lit inside. In recent years the house has been restored as a holiday cottage, boasting some of the most spectacular views on the whole of the Northumberland coast.

Continue along the path, which follows the cliff top, bearing left around the lip of a rocky bay; here the path leads through a wicket gate and meets the Craster road, but keep to the path, which runs parallel with the road. Soon after the coastal path bears right away from the road, it passes through a wicket gate and continues along the cliff top.

Gorse, elder and blackthorn thickets crouch in the dips out of the wind and the path tunnels through them before leading out beside Swine Den and Cullernose Point. The cliff face of Cullernose is dolerite, a grey volcanic rock pushed up or squeezed between sandstone and shale sediments nearly 300 million years ago. Unlike sandstone, the dolerite is very hard; wind and rain make no impression. However, pieces that fall into the sea are rounded and smoothed and rubbed against each other, then dumped by storms onto the beach of the Swine Den, where they may look like a herd of sleeping pigs.

Cullernose Point is ahead on the right. The white birds sitting on the ledges are likely to be kittiwakes, although occasionally there are fulmars too. Kittiwakes are small oceanic gulls that spend most of their time out at sea, except during the breeding

Cullernose Point: a favourite haunt for nesting fulmars

season when they come ashore to nest on small ledges on precipitous cliffs such as those here at Cullernose or on the nearby Farne Islands. They spend the first few years of their life in the western Atlantic between Greenland and Newfoundland, only returning to the cliffs where they were born when they are about three years old and ready to breed.

Go through another wicket-gate and over the brow of the gorse bank, called Long Heugh, bearing right on the close-cropped grass and keeping well clear of the fence along the cliff edge. Head downhill, towards the sea and Cullernose Point.

The rocks of Cullernose Point are a favourite place for sea-anglers. They cast over the swell, where the tide hits a submerged shelf of whinstone, and use lug or ragworm to catch wrass or pollack. During the winter they fish for cod, up to 25lb. in weight.

The path turns left over the grassy pasture, heading north towards Craster, with Dunstanburgh Castle in the distance. Just before the village, the path skirts around two little rocky bays. On the far side, go through a wicket gate and follow a narrow path beside some garden walls, then keep to the right of the children's play area to continue along the path above the rocky shoreline. Through a wicket gate, cross the beer garden of the Jolly Fisherman pub to another wicket. Here, turn left up towards the kippering sheds, then right down the road into the village.

Craster kippers are world famous - and justly so, they are delicious, especially barbecued. The kippering sheds were built in the mid 19th century and are still used for smoking herring, as well as cod and salmon, all of which can be bought in the shop attached to the smokehouse. Until the mid 1990s, the herring were caught off the Northumberland Coast by local fishing boats that docked at Craster harbour. With the collapse of North Sea fish stocks, the herrings smoked in Craster now have to be imported from Iceland and Norway.

The little harbour, built by the Craster family, usually has cobles or inshore boats pulled up onto its shore and there are stacks of crab and lobster pots to add a touch of atmosphere (they always smell fishy and attract the gulls). Boats entering the harbour look for the signal on the north pier; a green or red flag for go or stop, and a black and white one for heave to and wait.

From the harbour, walk left on the main road out of the village, then after about 200 metres turn left into a car park beside the Tourist Information Centre.

The level area of the car park through to the left past the Information Centre is the site of a whinstone quarry, where quartz-dolerite was extracted and crushed to make roadstone or cut into blocks for kerbstones. An overhead cableway linked the quarry with the harbour-mouth. It was a big, noisy and dusty operation and when the quarry finally closed, fifty years ago, fishing became the main local employment.

Quarry scars are sometimes slow to heal, but plants soon covered the moist sheltered soil below the whinstone ridge. Trees and bushes established themselves and migrant birds such as whitethroats and blackcaps began to move in. Soon the site was unrecognisable as a quarry and was turned by the Northumberland Wildlife Trust into a nature reserve, dedicated to the memory of Dr. Lawrence Arnold. Display panels close to the Information Centre describe what can be seen in the immediate area.

Take the woodland path to the right, running just behind the Tourist Information Centre and signed 'Craster South Farm ½'. Follow the path through the wood and go through the wicket gate at the very end of the path (some 50 metres after passing by a first wicket gate on the right hand side). This leads out onto a field along a clearly defined grass path up the hill.

The path crosses ancient field systems, now covered with grass. To the left are terraces running parallel to the path, to the right (and running at right angles) are rigg and furrow marks created by centuries of ploughing. Craster Tower, which would have been the hub of the ancient estate, lies hidden among the trees to the right as you approach Craster South Farm. There may have been a wooden palisade on the spot in Norman times but by 1415 this had been replaced by a stone tower or pele. This still survives, incorporated into a Georgian house and with fashionable Gothic alterations. The word Craster comes from 'Craucestr', the settlement or fort of the crows, and it is quite possible that the tall trees have always been a nesting place for rooks.

Go through the wicket gate at the end of the field and cross the road (TAKE CARE!), heading up a tarmac track, signed 'Howick Hall Gates', beside Craster South Farm. Past the row of cottages, bear left along a grass track, with a hedge to the left and an open field to the right.

Yellowhammers are common birds of arable farmland. Corn buntings, recognised by their larger size and key-jangling song, have all but disappeared over the last twenty years. Any other buntings seen near the coast are likely to be winter vagrants such as Lapland and snow buntings. To the right on the skyline is Alnwick Moor and the Cheviot. To the left is the back of Long Heugh, part of the same dolerite ridge that forms Cullernose Point. The gap in the ridge is a meltwater channel, created in the Ice Age by water boring an escape-course beneath the sheet of ice.

The hedge is replaced by a low wall and a fence: keep alongside these to a wicket gate beside a finger post. Through this, go half-right and follow an indistinct grassy path signed to 'Howick Hall' running below the gorse covered crags of Hips Heugh.

A heugh is the local name for the abrupt little ridges that mark the Whin Sill in this area. Whin or gorse bushes on the Whin Sill do not attract whinchats, which despite the name are more likely to be found on bracken-covered banks. But Hips Heugh's gorse does suit stonechats and they announce themselves with a very sharp call, like clicking stones together.

Past two lone sycamore trees, and with the ridge of Hips Heugh to the left, the path bears right to a ladder-stile and wicket gate in a stone wall. Cross the stile and follow a path half-left over the field. The path is sometimes not very distinct, but make for the gate at the left-hand end of the wood opposite. Go through the gate and follow the field-edge track, with the wood to your right.

The wood, grown up along the course of a burn, hides a steading called Peep o' Sea just to the north of Howick Hall. The trees are sycamore, oak, ash, beech and sweet chestnut, and in the spring their mossy roots are covered with drifts of snowdrops and daffodils. A little later, wild flowers such as dog's mercury, wood anemone and red campion also thrive on the shaded banks of the burn.

At the end of the field, the track bears right to cross a burn (often hidden by undergrowth) then climbs a short rise before meeting the access track to Howick Hall Car Park and leading out onto a road.

Howick Hall Gardens are open to the public and there are miles of woodland paths to explore if you feel like a detour. If not, turn left down the road, along the pavement beside a line of beech trees. At the next road junction, keep straight on, not left along the side-road signed to Howick village. The sea is straight ahead. As the road bears sharp left, turn right, back to the start.

5. Craster & Dunstanburgh Castle

THE BATTLE-SCARRED RUINS of Dunstanburgh Castle and some Second World War pillboxes are a reminder of how much a good view has been valued over the years. Heughs, low ridges of dark volcanic rock topped by a blazing quilt of gorse, are a feature of the coast and make good vantage points.

This is an attractive farmland walk of about 4½ miles, following the dip and scarp slopes of a very distinctive heugh. The walk starts from the little harbour at Craster and heads north, on a grassy path above the shore, past mighty Dunstanburgh and the old dunes of Embleton Bay, then back across the fields, following farm tracks into the shade of the whinstone ridge.

Park in the Tourist Information Centre car park on the edge of Craster village. Turn right and walk down the road to the harbour.

The rear section of the car park makes use of an old whinstone quarry; 'whin' is the local name for dolerite, the dark grey volcanic rock that outcrops along the Northumberland coast in the form of heughs or ridges. Whinstone is very hard and for many years it was extracted and shipped out for use as sets, cobbles and road chippings. Unfortunately, the fine-grained structure of the rock means that, although it is hard-wearing, it eventually becomes as smooth and slippery as glass (which is why it is dangerous to walk on sea-weathered rocks). In its heyday over sixty years ago the whinstone from this quarry was carried by overhead cableway to the harbour for shipping out to other parts of the country; the concrete block at the end of the south pier is what remains of the loading hopper. Over the last few decades the quarry site has been claimed back by nature; the woodland and thorn thickets have become an important refuge for migrant songbirds such as the whitethroat and chiffchaff.

Craster harbour and village

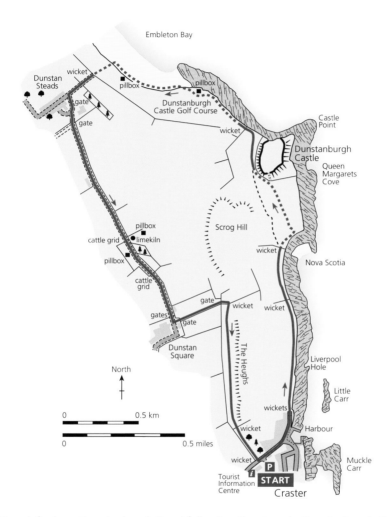

Turn left along Dunstanburgh Road following the signs to Dunstanburgh Castle.

The harbour was built in 1906 by the Craster family to service their quarries and the local fishing fleet of twenty or thirty cobles. There is a commemorative plaque dedicated to the memory of Captain Craster who died on the Tibetan Expedition of 1904. In fact, the Crasters have had a long and honourable military history; two were at Agincourt and another was Constable of Dunstanburgh.

One or two cobles still fish the inshore waters from Craster and can often be seen hauled up on the shore. Herring, the life blood of North Sea fishing, is now an endangered species and so is the associated industry. However, Craster has always been famous for its kippers and there is still a smoke-house in the village where herring, as well as salmon and cod, are smoked in the traditional way over oak sawdust: they are all delicious and can be bought at the small shop attached to the smokehouse.

At the end of the road, go through two wicket gates and follow the coast path northwards, signed 'Public Footpath – Dunstanburgh Castle 1¼'.

Gorse usually makes a dramatic show on the bank above the shore. The cadmium-yellow of the flowers can be dazzling (seashore and mountain flowers are noted for their bright colours because of the higher UV content in the light). The local name for gorse is whin; it is possible that whinstone gets its name from the whin-covered hills of the Northumberland coast.

To the right, the pasture tilts down to a shoreline of bare dolerite. The markers on the exposed rocks of Little Carr are there to guide boats into the harbour. On the far side of the harbour entrance is Muckle Carr (i.e. big rocks).

Continue along the grassy path. At the small inlet of Nova Scotia the path takes a gentle curve to the right and then bears sharp left up a long slope towards the castle.

It is hard to concentrate on anything else when Dunstanburgh Castle is brooding on the skyline. When the castle was built, around 1313, the little bay of Nova Scotia was an inlet extending to the marshy ground to the left. It was just wide enough to provide a safe harbour, and in 1514 a fleet of Henry VIII's warships took refuge here. Much later, in 1958, a Polish trawler was stranded in the bay and its wreck is still visible at low tide.

At the entrance gate to the castle, bear left along a narrow path around the hillside, keeping the fence to the right.

Facing Dunstanburgh from the south, the most obvious feature is the keep (the original gatehouse). On the far right is the Egyncleugh Tower ('Margaret's Tower'), which overlooks a hidden chasm called the Rumbling Churn ('Queen Margaret's Cove'). Queen Margaret was the resourceful and resolute wife of Henry VI, defeated at the battle of Hexham Levels in 1468. She made her escape from here in a fishing boat.

The castle was built too late to be of any strategic value in the Border Wars, but it saw some action as a Lancastrian stronghold in the Wars of the Roses. It was besieged, taken and retaken five times. Unfortunately, artillery had been invented by this time and the castle was soon a shattered hulk.

It must have been at about this time that Sir Guy the Seeker took refuge in the ruins one night and was invited by a flame-haired wizard to release a beautiful maiden from a spell and gain a sizable treasure. He was taken to a crystal tomb where the maiden lay in a trance, guarded by two giant skeletons and a hundred sleeping knights. The wizard offered Sir Guy a choice, of a horn or a sheathed sword. He chose the horn, woke up the knights rather than the maiden, and the whole scene vanished. His ghost, of course, still walks the ruins trying to find the maiden's chamber. The only substance to the legend is the treasure of Dunstanburgh diamonds (quartz crystals formed in the cracks of the dolerite) which still litter the site.

Continue around to the north side of the castle, then follow the coast path as it turns left above the rocky shoreline.

Dunstanburgh looks quite different from here. The dominant feature is the Lilburn Tower, which resembles a Norman keep, and instead of seeming to rest on a grassy knoll the castle actually sits above a vertical cliff. This is Gull Crag, the summer haunt of kittiwakes: sea-going gulls with yellow beaks and black wing-tips. They plaster their seaweed nests onto the bare rock and then whitewash the whole cliff with their droppings, which imparts a distinctive character to the place.

The top half of Gull Crag is dolerite and the rest is sandstone and shale. Across the boulder-lined shore is the Saddle Rock, made up of sediments of limestone buckled by the intrusion of the molten dolerite.

Go through a wicket-gate onto Dunstanburgh Castle Golf Course. Watch out for golfers driving to the green on the left. Follow the path to the right of the green and, after crossing a small hollow, continue along the dune ridge into Embleton Bay. If the tide is out, drop down onto the beach at the end of the rocks and walk along the high tide line.

Embleton Bay is one of the most beautiful bays in England. The dunes along this section of the coast are part of a Site of Special Scientific Interest are very important for wild flowers such as bloody cranesbill, cowslip and burnet rose - the most prickly and heavenly-scented of all wild roses. During the Second World War the bay was defended by machine-gun platforms and pill-boxes and several of these survive. In fact, the possibility of invasion, or at least a raid, must have been taken very seriously; Dunstanburgh was used as a look-out post and minefields were laid across the adjacent pastures. In the event, the only local action involved an enemy aircraft which shot at the soldiers laying the mines.

About 100 metres after the second pill-box, where the path dips down into a deeper cut in the dunes, turn left and head inland towards the buildings of Dunstan Steads. Go through the wicket-gate at the edge of the golf course and walk up the road towards the farm. Just before the farm, turn left along the tarmac driveway (signed as a cycle route to Craster) in front of the stone holiday cottages. As the drive curves to the right at the end of the cottages, bear left to a gate and onto a long straight concrete track with a hedge to the left and open fields to the right.

Wire fences and big open fields of winter barley, wheat and silage make for a dull section of walk. This is an impoverished stretch of countryside for wildlife, and it does no justice to the superb coastal scenery within the Northumberland Coast Area of Outstanding Natural Beauty.

Continue south along the track, over a cattle grid and past the remains of an old lime kiln on the left among pine trees.

Lime kilns were widespread in the 18th and 19th centuries and, although their architecture varied, the principle was usually the same. A low hill was required with one gently sloping side and one steep face. The kiln was corbelled into the face. Limestone from a nearby quarry was carted up the gentle slope and unloaded into a

Birdsfoot trefoil thrives on the thin whinstone soils

World War II pill box, beside the track to Dunstan Square

hole in the top. After burning, the resulting slaked lime, a white powder, was shovelled out of the side and bagged up, to be spread on fields to fertilise or sweeten the ground.

War time pill-boxes put in another appearance on the flanks of the wooded knoll, working as a pair to cover the whole sweep of country and hold back an army. They are well-preserved considering they were only used for a year or two and have been derelict for more than half a century. These two look like they were an economy version, being built by stacking hessian sacks filled with concrete, then topped with a concrete slab and covered in turf to disguise them from enemy aircraft.

Eventually the track reaches the farm at Dunstan Square. Go through two gates set a few metres apart (often left open) then turn left through another gate. Walk down the wide grassy path (signed 'Public Footpath – Craster 1 Dunstanburgh Castle 1¼') and make for the gap in the ridge ahead.

The gap is called The Shaird and it is a natural nick in the whinstone heugh, separating Scrog Hill from The Heughs. Gorse covers the entire ridge and is a haven for yellowhammers and linnets.

Go through the gate at the bottom of the field, then after 50 metres turn right through a wicket-gate and follow the grass path along the foot of The Heughs.

After about a kilometre you will reach a wicket gate, close to the base of the gorse covered slope. Continue, through an area of rough grassland and scrub, back to the Craster road then turn left to return to the car park.

6. Newton-by-the-Sea & Football Hole

THE TWIN HEADLANDS of Newton Point and The Snook separate wide sweeps of sand and guard one of the prettiest bays on the whole coast. This short easy walk of just over 2½ miles drops down into Low Newton village before following the grassy coast path northwards around the point to Football Hole and The Snook, then turning south on the corner of Beadnell Bay and following a quiet country lane back through High Newton.

The coastal section of the walk between Low Newton and Newton Links House crosses land that is owned by the National Trust and follows a permissive route that is used with their consent. The dunes and coastal grasslands are very important for wildlife and visitors are asked to help avoid damage to the vegetation by keeping to the path.

Park in the Northumberland County Council Car Park, at grid reference NU 239248, on the right before the road drops down into Low Newton. Walk towards the village. About 50 metres before the road ends there is a wicket gate on the left.

Low Newton-by-the-Sea, or Newton Seahouses as it was once known, is a modest little fishing village taking advantage of a natural harbour or haven. Carrs or rock spits keep out any storm-driven seas and boats can be pulled out onto the beach. The old part of the village comprises a three-sided terrace of stone-built cottages with a public house, 'The Ship' (a pleasant spot for a pint and a pub lunch) tucked into one of the corners. A detour around the back of the square leads to a public hide with views over Newton Pool Nature Reserve.

Immediately through the wicket gate close to the road end, take the path to the right that runs above the rocky shoreline (not the path half-left heading uphill and signed to 'Beadnell').

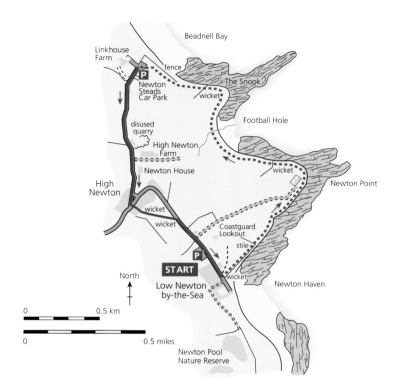

Dunstanburgh Castle dominates the sky-line, as it was intended to do when Edmund, Earl of Lancaster first thought about building a fortress here towards the end of the 13th century. He gained the land from Simon de Montford but left it to his son Thomas to get the job done. Thomas had fallen out with Edward II and was in need of protection. The ruined castle shows its best profile from here, silhouetted against the light. From the grassy path, a shelf of rock slopes down into the sea. Bands of lichen, black Verrucaria and orange Caloplaca, mark salt or sea tolerance zones above high water.

Cross the stile over an old drystone wall, and if the tide is low, drop down to follow the rock shelf to a tiny bay.

The bay is only about 50 metres wide and has no name, but it makes a perfect picnic place and is protected from prevailing winds. The boulder-beach is worth checking for lucky hag-stones (rocks with holes worn through them: a twist of wire through the hole turns a stone into a protection against witches).

Continue along the grassy path towards the headland of Newton Point.

Sunrise over Newton Haven

Football Hole and Cowslips on Newton Point

The slope of close-cropped grass down to Newton Point is good for celandines and cowslips, short-stemmed to keep them out of the wind. Cowslips thrive on old pastures, often grazed by cattle: the name cowslip comes from 'cow-slop', meaning the plant had a reputation for growing where cow-pats had fertilised the ground.

After Newton Point, continue around the headland, making for the wide sandy bay of Football Hole. Go through the wicket-gate in the old stone wall and, after about 150 metres, either walk down to follow the shoreline or keep to the dune path, depending on the state of the tide.

Football Hole is a gem, one of the most picturesque places on the east coast, rarely visited and totally unspoilt. The beach slopes sharply offshore, which makes it a dangerous place to paddle, and on a rising tide the breakers can be fierce and deafeningly loud. This makes it even more special: a good place to talk to the sea.

Just beyond the headland of The Snook, go through the wicket-gate in the fence and follow the dune path, with the wide expanse of Beadnell Bay ahead. On the far side of a hollow in the dunes, keep to the dune-top path to the left of a fence.

As you approach Linkhouse Farm (surrounded by trees) bear left away from the dune ridge and head down to a stile on the south side of Newton Steads Car Park. Through the car park, turn left along the road which takes you past a row of farm cottages, High Newton Farm and Newton House.

At the village of High Newton, instead of cutting back sharp left down the road to Low Newton, cross the green with the Joiners' Arms on the right and take the waymarked public footpath (signed 'Low Newton-by-the-Sea') sandwiched between the modern bungalows and the high stone wall. Cross the field to the road.

The pasture is just as much a piece of mediaeval history as Dunstanburgh Castle. Ridge and furrow marks are not so easy to date, but they usually show where an open field system was worked. The profile of humps and hollows was deliberately built up over the years by always ploughing in the same direction, casting the furrows to the centre and creating a shaped mound. The reason for the centuries of effort is lost in the mists of time, but it was probably something to do with improving drainage or increasing the surface area of the ground. Old field systems like this one have S-shaped ridges because the heavy ploughs had to be pulled by long teams of oxen; they needed a curve to be able to turn round at the headlands. The path has stone bed and has been built across the lines of the ridge and furrow.

At the wicket-gate turn right and follow the road back to the car park.

The white building on the brow of the hill, at its closest now but visible almost every step of the way, is the old coastguard lookout. The tall radio mast has replaced any watchers, but one of the cottages is still kept as a sub-broadcast station to store equipment and relay messages. These days most coastguard work is done by beacons.

Newton Haven

7. Seahouses, Monks House & Shoreston

BY BEACH AND DUNE PATH from the fishing harbour of Seahouses past Monks House to Greenhill, then back along field paths and tracks, via Shoreston Hall to North Sunderland. About 5 miles, the walk is perfect as a complement to a half-day boat trip around the Farne Islands, which start from Seahouses. It offers the best shore views of the islands and gives an unusual perspective on the farmland backing the dunes.

Park in the town centre car park in Seahouses, opposite the war memorial. Turn left out of the car park, cross over to the seaward side of the main road and continue north, with the sea to your right. Follow the grassy path along the cliff top above the beach, taking care to keep well back from the edge.

The seashore is rocky at first, with beds of sedimentary rock buckled into roller-coaster waves nearly 300 million years ago, towards the end of the hot, swampy Carboniferous Period when molten rock was pushed up between the existing layers of limestone and sandstone. 'The Tumblers' is an appropriate name for this particular jumble of rocks.

Looking back, there is a good view of the entrance to Seahouses Harbour. From Easter onwards there will be a regular traffic of passenger boats, to and from the Farne Islands and, depending on the time and tide, there may be trawlers plying between regular fishing grounds in the North Sea.

At the beginning of St Aidan's Dunes take the steps leading down onto the beach and walk along the high tide mark.

Seahouses harbour

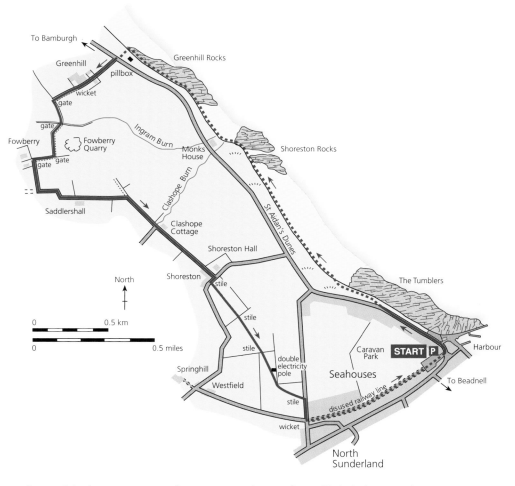

Some of the huge concrete tank stops, set in place to thwart Hitler's threatened invasion, have disappeared beneath the dunes. Others have reappeared as the mobile dunes have been shifted landward by the wind. Where lyme grass and marram have anchored the ground more firmly, behind the storm beach and out of the worst of the spray, flowers such as burnet rose can be found. Most wild roses are a disappointment; they look spectacular for a few days but have a poor scent. With the little burnet rose the opposite is true; they grow just a foot or so tall, have cream flowers rather than red or pink, yet have a wonderful fragrance.

After about half a mile there is another outcrop of rocks, Shoreston Rocks, on the lower beach. Bear left along the tideline around the next headland. Monks House comes into view for the first time, tucked into a recess in the dunes.

Monks House is actually three houses gathered together in a sheltered nook along the dunes. Apart from the main house there is Brock Burn, named after the little stream, which is itself named after the resident badgers, and Brownsman Cottage which is a converted stable and is named after one of the Farne Islands. The original Monks House began as a storehouse, granted by Henry III in 1257 to the Monks of Farne and built next to his 'Mill of Brocksmouth'. The monks soon added a ferry house to the granary, and by the end of the fifteenth century there was a garden, chapel and probably a graveyard too. Most of this must have disappeared under the dunes with the Dissolution of the Monasteries.

The present buildings were rescued and renovated in 1949 and made into one of Britain's first bird observatories by the wildlife artist Eric Ennion. He was an inspirational figure and a pioneer of the Field Studies movement; many a young naturalist (Bill Oddie and John Busby, to name but two) passed through Monks House in the ten years it was operational. The only reminders of its days as an observatory are the weather vane, in the shape of a long-tailed duck, and a list of rare bird sightings which includes a lesser grey shrike and a Pallas' warbler, both seen in the sycamore tree in the garden.

Cross the Clashope and Ingram Burns below Monks House, either by wading (they are often both very shallow) or by crossing the small ford and sleeper footbridge immediately in front of the gardens.

Monks House and the Ingram Burn

Boat trips to the Farnes leave from Seahouses harbour

The fresh water and rock outcrops always make this a good place for wading birds; never very many of each, but usually several different sorts. Grey and ringed plover, bar-tailed godwit, curlew, redshank, turnstone, purple sandpiper and sanderling are the species most likely to be seen, whatever the time of year. Only the ringed plover nests nearby, among pebbles on the upper beach. In the days when Monks House was a bird observatory several ingenious traps were invented to catch and ring the waders on the shore.

Continue around the next headland above Greenhill Rocks or, if the tide is high, take a path up onto the dunes and walk along the dune ridge.

This is as close as you can get to the Farne Islands without a boat. Inner Farne, the biggest of the fifteen proper islands (another thirteen appear at low tide) is less than two miles away. In the summer, white clouds of kittiwakes and arctic terns swirl around the cliff tops and lighthouse. Guillemots and puffins are more difficult to spot: a boat trip to the more distant Staple Island is thoroughly recommended.

Between the islands and the shore is Inner Sound. On still days it is worth looking for grey seals, which like to loaf about and watch people from the safety of the sea. Fins breaking the surface may be a dolphin or a killer whale, and at very low tides the tail of a crashed Lancaster bomber sometimes appears.

About 50 metres past the old World War II pill-box perched high up on the dunes, and as Greenhill Rocks come to an end, cut left off the beach up a dune path: this leads to the Bamburgh - Seahouses road.

From the road, Bamburgh Castle appears for the first time, a solid fortress set square on a heugh or whinstone ridge. What remains is the result of regular rebuilding, most recently in Victorian times, and the oldest visible structure is the Norman Keep. But

Bamburgh had earned a place in history much earlier, as Dinguvaroy, the castle of the first Northumbrian king, Ida the Flamebearer. This was in 547 and the castle was probably no more than a wooden hall with a palisade around it. It was described at the time as having been protected by a hedge, the first reference in history to such a boundary. Ida's grandson Ethelfrith gave the place to his queen, Bebba, which is how it became Bebbanburgh and eventually Bamburgh.

Taking care to watch out for traffic (its a fast road!), cross over and head up the access track to Greenhill Farm.

In the 18th and 19th centuries many farms were the size of hamlets or villages, with rows of cottages for the workers and extensive sheds and hemmels for the animals. Here, the cottages have been turned into holiday lets and even bigger sheds have been built to allow better access for tractors. Modern farmers have had to invest in capital equipment rather than in people or the land.

At the end of the track between the farm buildings, go through the wicket-gate into the field and walk straight ahead to the next gateway. Go through this (please close the gates behind you), turn sharp left and follow the wall. At the bottom of the field, bear right to cross the Ingram Burn and go through a gate.

The little burn is covered over by brambles and briars, providing a refuge for warblers and buntings. The fields to the left, towards Monks House which is now visible along the valley of the burn, used to be very marshy and attracted waders and wildfowl, but the course of the burn has been straightened and the fields drained to allow crops to be grown.

Fowberry Quarry, eaten into the hillside on the left and now hidden amongst the gorse, was dug out in the eighteenth century to provide building stone for Fowberry Farm.

Follow the path beside the hedge, then bear right through a gate and continue to Fowberry Farm. At the farm, turn left up the narrow road; it bears left, then winds between hedge-banks and fences, past Saddlershall towards the hamlet of Shoreston.

The track might be an old one but the limited variety of plants in the hedges (hawthorn with a few elder, gooseberry and honeysuckle) suggests that they were planted in the last century. The rolling cornfields are at their best in early green leaf or close to harvest, when the colours of the distant sea, dunes, hedges and the shoals of corn look as if they have been mixed by Matisse.

At Clashope Cottage keep straight on to Shoreston, ignoring the turn to the right.

There are estate walls on either side of the track, covered with lichens (Lecanora white, Xanthoria yellow) and with patches of stinging nettle to provide food-plants for small tortoiseshell and red admiral butterflies. Beyond the wall on the left is a horse pasture showing old rigg and furrow marks, meaning that it has been under cultivation of some sort for several centuries.

At the T-junction in Shoreston turn right, then after about 15 metres turn left over a stone stile, signed to 'North Sunderland'. Walk along the path, straight across the field, heading for a stile in the far fence-line. Cross this into another field. The farmer usually has a crop growing but, with walkers trampling a path, the line of the path is clear most of the time: if not, head straight across, aiming for the stile in the fence-line opposite, just to the right of the double electricity pole silhouetted against the North Sunderland skyline.

Go over the stile, cross the field diagonally left, making for the double pole, then keep slightly right of the poles and at the hedge corner bear left over the open field. Make for the stile at the end of a stone wall, where it joins a hedge and in line with two large sheds of the local garage. Over the stile, turn right along the road.

After about 150 metres cross the road and turn left through a wicket-gate to follow a tree-lined path along the bed of an old railway line. This leads back, past a caravan site, to the main car park.

The branch-line, from Chathill, was closed in the early 1950s but its legacy of a walkway has mellowed with the years and is popular with local dogs, spring flowers and willow warblers.

Alternatively, continue along Broad Road to the White Swan Hotel, then turn left and walk along the main road through North Sunderland and back to the Seahouses car park.

A storm brewing off Seahouses

47

8. Bamburgh Castle & Budle Point

IN THE SHADOW OF A GREAT FORTRESS but taking in views of the most spectacular sweep of sea and sand on the whole coast. Just over 4 miles and easy walking, round the north side of the castle, along the shore and then up the dunes and around the edge of a golf course. The wind usually blows, rain can squall in from any direction, but there are a surprising number of days when the sun beams down from a cloudless sky and the sea is Mediterranean blue. The last mile is along a road verge, but with a path alongside and lots to see along the way.

Park in the large car park opposite the castle. Cross the road and climb the access track around the right (south) side of the castle, watching out for oncoming traffic exiting from the castle car park.

The castle was tailored to fit the shape of the whinstone ridge, not perched on the top so much as extending upwards out of the solid rock. Fulmars accept the artificial nest-sites graciously and spend a lot of their time, in and out of the breeding season, sitting on the shelves and sills of the south wall. Most crevices are carpeted with wallflowers, which act as a scented carpet for what are, in fact, very smelly birds.

Cross over the castle car park and bear left down a narrow path leading around the seaward side of the castle. Continue along the path, keeping left through a deep cutting in the dunes, and head for the crag at the north corner of the Castle rock.

The broad band of dunes between the castle and the beach is criss-crossed by a thousand paths. A great bleached scoop out of the heart of one of the biggest dunes shows what happens when the wind really gets a hold; tons of sand can be swept up and carried away or moulded into a new spit or ridge. Covering dunes is a speciality of marram grass but many a battle is lost against winter storms.

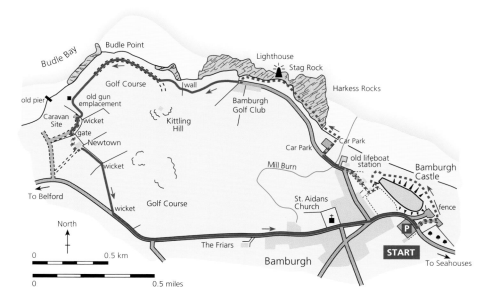

On the left the columns and faces of rock below the castle are covered with frondose lichens and patches of wallflower. Dense patches of ivy and polypody fern trail over the banks and on sunny days the big hairy caterpillars of drinker and garden tiger moths sit out on the bare edges of the path. Apart from the obvious risk of being trodden on they are safe from most danger; the only creature to make a habit of eating them, hair and all, is the cuckoo.

At the end of the Castle, just beyond a high rock face, take the path left that curves gently uphill, with the stump of the old Castle windmill high up to your left. Keep left to go through the gap between two high stone walls and follow the path around to the right along the edge of the sports field. Just beyond the pavilion, turn right along a grass path past Coastguard Cottages to meet a road at the old lifeboat station (now called 'The Boathouse')

The lintel and filled-in doorway on the gable-end of the house show that it really was a lifeboat station. In fact it was the first to be built in Britain, in the early 1820s, and it served for many years until a much bigger boat and station was established at Seahouses. When needed, the Bamburgh boat was pulled out onto the track and wheeled down to be launched from the beach.

Follow the road to the right, past the entrance to a car park and over the Mill Burn. At the brow of the first hill, turn right into a car park and cross the narrow band of dunes down to the beach. Turn left and make your way towards the lighthouse on Harkess Rocks. If the tide is out, walk along the rocks beneath the grass bank; if not, climb the bank and continue west along the roadside.

49

Bamburgh Castle

The lighthouse is automatic and only needs occasional maintenance. Gone are the days of lighthouse-keepers, even for the Longstone at the far tip of the Farne Islands. The dazzling whiteness of the Stag Rock lighthouse is an important design feature, so it can be seen from miles around and, when the building is repainted, the white stag on the nearby rocks also gets a fresh coat. The artistic rendering varies year by year: sometimes it even looks like a stag.

The face of rock on which the stag is painted is quartz-dolerite, again part of the Whin Sill which was forced or 'intruded' into the existing sandstone and limestone sediments 295 million years ago. The magma was pushed into layers of existing rock like hot jam being squirted into a sandwich cake; any limestone close to the dolerite was baked hard and turned to marble. A band of this metamorphosed rock can be seen to the left of the stag.

In the autumn and winter, in the very worst of weathers, Stag Rock becomes popular with bird-watchers. On-shore gales drive seabirds close inshore and it is possible to see skuas, shearwaters and gannets passing a few metres away rather than miles out. Sitting for an hour or more in the teeth of an easterly gale is not for the faint-hearted; sea-watching sorts out those who really want to 'twitch' a rarity.

At the lighthouse, pause to take a rest; sit on the wooden bench and enjoy the view. Keep to the left of the lighthouse and continue along the path at the base of the grass bank. After about 250 metres and level with the clubhouse of Bamburgh Castle Golf Club (all you will be able to see from the path is a small white cabin and the flagpole), turn left to ascend the path to the road.

At the top of the bank turn right (signed 'Budle Point ¾') to go through a white painted wicket gate beside the first tee. As instructed by the notice on the gate, follow the route of the right of way as indicated by the blue tipped marker posts. (Take Care: Watch out for golf balls). For the first few hundred metres the path crosses the golf course but then bears right through a gap in an old stone wall to run along the top of the grassy bank high above the beach. Further on towards Budle Point this continues as a wide stony track.

A tramway used to link the whinstone quarry at Kittling Hill with a pier down on the shore. Whin chips were in demand for roadstone, dispatched by boat far and wide. The track is the bed of the old tramway, covered with a sample of the chips.

There can be few better views on the Northumberland coast than the curve of Ross Back Sands, leading the eye from Budle Bay to Holy Island. If the tide is out there will be an endless shoal of white sand, deserted apart from a few cormorants gathered on the point of Budle Water to dry their wings. The whole wilderness of sand is usually left to the birds; Ross Links is awkward to get to because there are no roads, and the wind usually makes the beach uncomfortable. Just offshore of Ross Back Sands is a shallow shelf called Skate Road, a favourite fishing ground for red-throated divers and Slavonian grebes.

Even the most inspiring view palls after a few years. The gun emplacement on Budle Point faces a narrow arc of the North Sea. Second World War gunners, weary of watching for an invasion that never came, must surely have felt tempted to blow a hole in Lindisfarne Castle.

Ahead in the distance are the Kyloe Hills. The Lammermuir Hills, well into Scotland, lie beyond. To the left, its whaleback summit visible over Spindlestone Heugh and the rise of Chatton Moor, is the Cheviot.

An incoming tide in Budle Bay

Follow the path left around the old gun emplacement, then sharp left up the bank onto the golf course. Following the blue posts, keep to the right of the green and tees and take a grass path to the right, to a wicket gate. This leads to a narrow metalled road with caravans to the right. Bear left along the road then, after 50 metres, turn sharp left through the gateway and up the track to Newtown.

The view north from here must be one of the best on the whole of the Northumberland Coast. Beyond the inlet of Budle Bay can be seen the vast expanse of Ross Back Sands, with Holy Island and Lindisfarne Castle in the far distance. I never tire of the sheer scale and simplicity of this view and would happily sit here for hours.

Cross the stone track behind the cottages and go straight ahead up the field towards a gate on the skyline. Go through the wicket gate onto the golf course and, turning half right, walk across the fairway towards the stone lookout, taking care to watch for golfers coming from the left. (The route of this footpath is also marked with blue posts.) Follow the path through the gorse a few metres to the left of the lookout and, still following the markers, continue across the golf course and make for the gate to the right of the green and tees at the end of the road-side post and rail fence.

Golf courses are surprisingly good for wildlife, particularly those situated close to the sea. The greens are cut and weeded but the roughs are a haven for flowers and insects. Drinker moth caterpillars are joined here in the spring by fox moth and ruby tiger caterpillars. Again, all are very hairy and like to sunbathe on the grass or heather stems. Predators may not be much of a problem but many caterpillars will have been attacked the previous autumn by parasitic wasps called Braconids. The grubs of the parasites feed within the bodies of their hosts until it is time for them to pupate, then they eat their way out and leave the poor caterpillars to die. Any shrunken or mummified caterpillars along the path in early summer will have suffered this nasty fate.

Go through the wicket-gate on the edge of the golf course. Turn left and walk along the wide roadside verge back to Bamburgh.

Road cuttings through the whinstone make impressive rock gardens. Most of the stone faces are draped with rust-coloured carpets of stonecrop and there are clumps of polypody and spleenwort ferns. Blue-flowered alkanet grows along the verge too, perhaps a sign that mediaeval monks had a herb garden nearby. The root of the plant was used to make a red dye as a local substitute for henna.

The first set of buildings marks the site of a Dominican Friary, though the area is also famous for its Augustinians and they made more of a mark on the history of the church and castle. Closer to the village on the left is the Parish Church of St. Aidan. Aidan was a monk from Iona, sent here at the request of King Oswald. Northumbria began its golden age with Oswald, who gained the throne and reunited the nation in 635 by defeating the pagan Cadwallon at the battle of Heavenfield, near Hexham. After his victory, Oswald invited Ionian monks to establish the Lindisfarne monastery and Aidan was their leader. Nothing remains of the wooden Anglo-Saxon church, except perhaps a beam over the baptistry, which is said to have been part of the original outer wall. Aidan died propped up against the beam, which is why it survived, miraculously, when everything else was raised to the ground.

The churchyard is the resting place of Grace Darling, the heroine of a famous Victorian sea rescue. She was the daughter of the Longstone's lighthouse keeper and helped him to save a crew of shipwrecked sailors from the Harcar Rock when their boat, the Forfarshire, was lost in a storm in 1838. Grace was a reluctant celebrity for the rest of her short life; she died aged 26, only four years after the rescue. Her grave is elaborate and inappropriate; a better way to appreciate her life and times, and the rescue itself, is to visit the RNLI museum on the other side of the road.

Walk into Bamburgh, past the village green, along the road towards the castle, and back to the car park.

St Aidans Church: the churchyard is the final resting place of Grace Darling

9. Holy Island

ISLANDS, big or small, are places of mystery and romance. Holy Island, the cradle of Christianity and culture in the Dark Ages, is now a place for picnics rather than pilgrims but every nook and cranny has a story to tell. This circuit of the eastern end of the island is a little over 3½ miles in length and takes about three hours; not only are there relics and ruins along the way, but the shoreline, wildlife and sea views can be breathtaking.

Holy Island is only cut off from the mainland for a few hours each day, but check the tides before crossing the causeway, to make sure you have enough time to complete the walk (see **www.lindisfarne.org.uk**). Whatever the time of year, or the weather, it is often more exciting to be on the island for high tide (if it rains you can visit the Priory or take refuge in the pub or tearoom).

The walk starts from the island's main car park on the left side of the road as you enter the village from the causeway.

From the car park, turn left along the main road, past the Lindisfarne Hotel, towards the centre of the village.

Holy Island has an international reputation for rare birds, especially in the late autumn when migrants from Scandinavia or Siberia are driven off course by bad weather. A 'fall' of migrant songbirds sometimes has these roadside gardens awash with disoriented blackcaps and redstarts, and a scattering of red-breasted flycatchers and other unusual chats and warblers. These days, rare birds gather flocks of 'twitchers' or bird-watchers who spend hours scanning the gardens.

At the T junction, turn right, then take an immediate left down the road signed to Lindisfarne Priory.

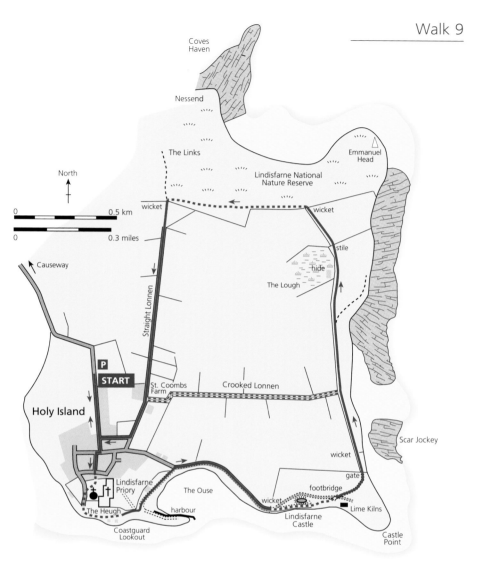

The Market Square lies at the heart of the village and has seen its share of excitement, particularly in the 19th century when there were ten inns serving a volatile community of fishermen and quarrymen. The surviving Crown and Anchor and the Manor House Hotel cater for different tastes, as does the nearby Lindisfarne Mead shop. The market cross dates back to 1828, but rests in a 16th century socket.

At the market cross, continue straight on, following the sign to the Priory. Past the Lindisfarne Priory Museum on the right, go through the gate into St. Mary's churchyard, then bear right along the grassy path between the gravestones and make for the gateway in the stone wall.

Across drifts of scurvy grass to the refuge box – for careless walkers caught by a rising tide - on the old Pilgrims Way between the mainland and Holy Island

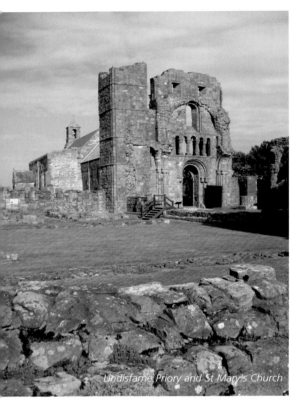
Lindisfarne Priory and St Mary's Church

The priory ruins are on the left as you enter the churchyard; they are in the care of English Heritage and there is an entry charge (payable at the excellent little Visitor Centre). However, the ruins can be viewed quite adequately from the (free) churchyard. The imposing arches and columns of the Norman priory date back to 1093, but by then the real glory days of Lindisfarne were long past. St Aidan had settled here from Iona in 635 and for two centuries his little monastery led Europe as a centre for Christian learning and culture. Viking raids in the 8th and 9th centuries put paid to Lindisfarne, the monks fleeing to the mainland before a final attack; they decided the island was no longer a safe refuge and they never returned.

At the end of the churchyard go through the gateway, turn left and continue down the winding track towards the sea.

A path to the right leads to the shore and to the old lifeboat house. The little offshore island, accessible at low tide, is called St Cuthbert's Island. Cuthbert was Bishop of Lindisfarne in the late 7th century and was the greatest and most celebrated of all the northern saints, possibly because he was also the most modest and self-effacing. After a spell as Prior of Lindisfarne, when he used this little island (then called Hobthrush) as a refuge for prayer and meditation, he left to become a hermit on Inner Farne. After nine years as a recluse he was finally persuaded by King Egfrid to return to the monastery as bishop - a position he held for just two years before his death in 687. When the monks finally left the island, St Cuthbert's body (miraculously preserved) was their greatest treasure. They took it with them, stuffing the Lindisfarne Gospels and a few of St Aidan's bones into the coffin for good measure.

Near the bottom of the hill, as the track curves to the right, turn left onto a grassy shelf and follow the path left up a stony bank to the top of The Heugh.

A heugh, pronounced 'he-uff', is a steep-sided ridge; on the Northumberland coast this usually means a volcanic dyke. The rock is a fine-grained dolerite, pushed up in a molten state through cracks and between layers of sediment. This happened nearly 300 million years ago: since then the sedimentary rocks have worn away leaving behind the harder volcanic rocks. Wild flowers do well in the crevices of the cliffs; sea campion, thrift, meadow saxifrage and sea plantain. Wallflower thrives too.

The Heugh is one of the highest points on the island and the panoramic view is excellent. It was from here, from the Chapel of the Lamps, that monks watched for the fires of marauding Scots in the 14th century.

To the south-east lie the Farne Islands (seven miles away) and Bamburgh Castle, whilst over the harbour is Guile Point on the tip of Ross Back Sands. The two tall beacons are navigation aids for a long-lost island fleet.

Walk past the former coastguard station and the war memorial, then follow the path left down to a group of fishery sheds. Bear left along a wide track with 'The Ouse' (the little harbour) to the right.

This place is always busy; it is a world of crab-creels, fishing nets and people painting boats or stripping down engines. If it looks untidy now, imagine it in the 1860s when the herring fishery was at its peak and there were over a hundred boats (mainly French) in the harbour. A traveller at the time complained that the landing-place was 'disgusting with filth, and it was difficult to approach the boats without treading on garbage'. Another noted 'the huge wooded vat round which the women stand to clean the herrings, and on the other side of the road fourteen hundred herring barrels in piles

Lindisfarne Castle and the old lime kilns from Castle Point

and rows.' It must have been a very smelly place. But the same writer also saw some of the fleet put to sea; 'The tide served, evening was coming on, and one after the other they hoisted sail, stood out of the bay, made a tack, some two tacks, and then away to the open sea.' A stirring sight.

The track meets a road as it makes its way eastwards from the village. Turn right along the road, towards the castle.

Lindisfarne Castle is tiny, but because it is perched on the top of another stretch of the dyke, called Beblowe Hill, it dominates the whole island. It was built in 1539 to defend the harbour approach but saw no action until 1715, when it was held for a day by Launcelot Errington and his nephew. They found the place virtually deserted and decided to claim it for the Jacobites, but left in a hurry when the garrison reappeared. A century later the castle was under the command of a bon viveur called Captain Rugg, described as 'a notable good fellow, as his great read nose ful of pimples did give testimony.'

Go through the gate at the end of the road and follow the cobbled track to the right of the castle. At the castle entrance, keep straight ahead past the upturned boats and to the left of a rocky knoll.

A traditional use for old boats on the island is to cut them up and make them into tool sheds: you will have seen several examples, in varying stages of decay, down by the harbour. The interpretive display in one of these three sections explains a little about their history.

The path soon drops down onto an old tramway to cross a timber footbridge: before doing so, it is worth taking a few minutes to have a look at the lime kilns over to your right.

The lime kilns were built in the 1860s by a Dundee firm. Limestone was brought here along the tramway from a quarry on the far side of the island, and coal was shipped in as fuel. The resulting slaked lime was then taken away to Scotland for use as fertiliser or mortar.

From the footbridge, continue along the raised tramway as it heads east and then curves north to a pair of gates above the rocks at Scar Jockey. Through the gates, keep to the grassy track, fence on the left and seashore on the right, for several hundred metres.

There is a footpath along a track to the left if you wish to take a short cut back to the village. The track is called the Crooked Lonnen. 'Lonnen' is an old dialect word for lane, and it is easy to visualise Celtic or Benedictine monks tending these fields.

Continue past the open water and marshland of 'The Lough'.

Right: Old stone beacons on Ross Back Sands that used to serve as navigation aids for boats entering Holy Island harbour

'Lough', pronounced 'loff', means a shallow lake. A public hide allows you to sit in comfort to see whatever birds are about. During the summer this is a far from peaceful place, with hundreds of nesting black-headed gulls. In winter there are teal, widgeon and families of whooper swans.

Past the bird hide, continue along the raised tramway to cross a stile in a fence line. A few hundred metres further on, go through a wicket gate onto Lindisfarne National Nature Reserve and turn sharp left along the path beside the stone wall.

The white pyramid marks Emmanuel Head, the north-east tip of the island. The dunes along this coast are wonderful for flowers such as grass of parnassus and marsh helleborine, and for butterflies like the common blue and the dark green fritillary. Skylarks fill the air, and rabbits, which were once one of the main crops on the island (raised in special coney warrens) are prolific. Before myxomatosis, rabbits were a useful supplement to the staple fish diet of island labourers, and there was a tradition of ferreting for them using crabs; a big 'dog-crab' had a lighted tallow candle fixed to the top of its shell and it was then sent down a burrow to bolt out the rabbits into waiting nets.

As the wall takes a right angle to the left, continue along the well-defined grassy path across tussocky ground. This leads to a junction with a wide lane (Straight Lonnen) heading south. A detour to the right leads through the dunes if you have time to explore the northern shore and the limestone quarries of Coves Haven. Neolithic flints have been discovered at Nessend, proving that people lived here thousands of years before the saints arrived. Otherwise, turn left and walk down Straight Lonnen towards the village. Eventually this leads past St Coombs Farm. About 200 metres past the farm, turn right beside the large sycamore tree (close to the car park for buses and disabled persons). At the T-junction, turn right along the main road and back to the car park.

10. Berwick Town Walls & Coast

BERWICKSHIRE and Berwick United Football Club are so solidly Scottish that it comes as a surprise to find Berwick upon Tweed, on the north side of the border river, still a part of England. Popular history has it that the town changed hands at least thirteen times in the Border Wars and there is evidence aplenty that for centuries the town was just waiting for the next attack. But this was long ago; if it were not for the unique Elizabethan town walls and fortifications Berwick would now be a pretty seaside town of bridges and painted stonework. This easy walk of about 3 miles takes to the ramparts, then out to the pier at the mouth of the Tweed. The return route follows the dramatic cliffs to the east of the town, back along the base of the walls for an invader's view of the defences.

Start at the Castlegate car park, just to the north of the Scotsgate archway.

At this point you are outside the walled town, but only just. The Elizabethan Ramparts rise above the car park, still solid and daunting. They are wonderfully preserved, perhaps because they were never called on to repulse an army. The northern and eastern walls and earthworks were built between 1558 and 1570 to link up with the mediaeval walls along the river frontage. The idea was to deter the Scots, who were then allied with France in doomed support of Mary Stuart. However, events passed Berwick by and a few years later the crowns were united under James I.

Walk to the car park entrance and turn left.

The road here is the old Great North Road, for centuries the life-line between London and Edinburgh. Facing you immediately is the Scotsgate, the main entrance to the town from the north.

Go through the pedestrian archway in the Scotsgate then turn left up the steps and along a tarmac path. A metal gate on the left takes you onto the Elizabethan Ramparts: from here the walk goes right, along the north wall of the ramparts, but take a few minutes to go left over the Scotsgate and climb Megs Mount.

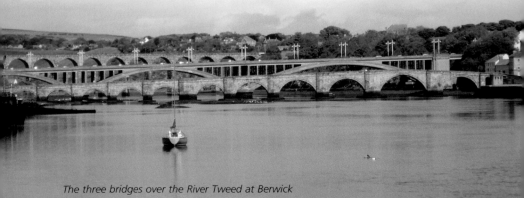

The three bridges over the River Tweed at Berwick

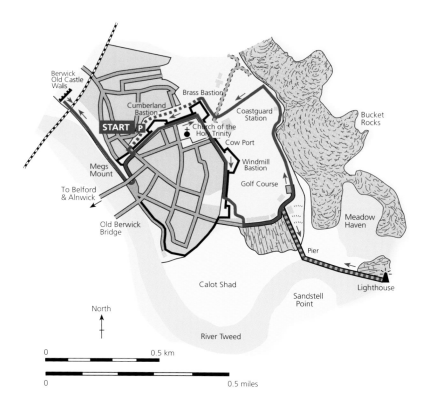

Megs Mount, an emplacement for a 'roaring meg' or cannon, occupies a commanding position at the north-west corner of the ramparts, overlooking the river approaches. The view is excellent; this is one of the best places to see Berwick's three bridges.

A short detour down the slope to the left of Megs Mount takes you along Bankhill, under the Royal Tweed Bridge (the new road bridge) to the 17th century Berwick Bridge and the old Quayside. By following the riverside path upstream for a few hundred yards it is also possible to walk beneath the Royal Border Bridge (the elegant railway bridge) and explore the ruins of Berwick Castle. This is where Edward I stayed on his way north to hammer the Scots; it is also where he held court and chose John Baliol to be his puppet king on the Scottish throne. The town paid for his bad judgment the following year (1292) when Edward had to send an army north to deal with Baliol's revolt; 7,000 Berwick people were massacred and the town was laid waste; until then it had been one of the wealthiest ports in Europe.

Retrace your route back to Scotsgate and walk along the ramparts to Cumberland Bastion.

The bastions, like the walls, were built of stone and filled with earth; functional rather than pretty. Their shape, like a blunt arrow-head, gave an all round field of fire, especially along adjacent sections of wall. On the far side of the Cumberland Bastion is an 18th century cannon, positioned in one of the flankers to demonstrate this strategy. The bastion is named after the Duke of Cumberland ('Butcher Cumberland') who passed through Berwick on his way to Culloden in 1745.

Continue to Brass Bastion at the north-eastern corner of the fortifications, then turn right (south) towards Windmill Bastion. To the right is the Parish Church of the Holy Trinity and St. Mary: for a closer look, take a short detour by following the path to the right just beyond Brass Bastion, then walk around the graveyard wall to the church entrance gate.

The architecture of the church is striking and unusual. It was completed in 1652 and was the only parish church to be built in England at the time of Cromwell's Commonwealth. Towers and steeples were considered frippery, the worst kind of moral decadence.

The dappled shade of the graveyard softens the lines of the church and the gravestones tell their own stories. One of the most poignant, which dates from the 19th century, must that of Thomas Statham Carpenter, his wife Elizabeth and their seven children, 'who all died in Minority'. Life was hard and could be very cruel.

On your way back to the ramparts from the church, take a look at the Cow Port, which passes through the walls between Brass Bastion and Windmill Bastion.

The Cow Port is the only surviving original gate through the ramparts, all others having been enlarged or altered since they were first built. The gate formerly consisted of an inner portcullis and an outer wooden door: the deep grooves which held the portcullis can still be seen in the stonework. Unfortunately, a strong gate is no defence if it is left open, which is what happened (by treachery) in 1318 when Robert Bruce took the town.

Back on the ramparts, continue south past Windmill Bastion towards the Magazine and the Lion House.

Windmill Bastion from the north

The Lion House and Magazine

As its name suggests, Windmill Bastion was once the site of a windmill. It must have cut an imposing figure on the skyline; an irresistible target for enemy artillery had there been any. Presumably the old mill was dismantled when the grass-topped mounds were added to the tops of the walls in the 17th century.

Beyond Windmill Bastion and set back from the ramparts is the 18th century Magazine or ammunition store. The thick and buttressed walls were intended to withstand stray artillery fire and to deflect any explosions upwards rather than sideways but, just to be on the safe side, it was still situated well away from the barracks and walls.

100 metres beyond the Magazine, take the railed steps down to the left through the ramparts and bear right along the tarmac path.

From this perspective the walls look frightening, half hidden behind wych elm and sycamore trees. But so in their day would the mediaeval defences which the path soon passes: all that remain are an embankment and ditch which can be seen on the left just before you reach the terrace of houses.

Where the path meets the terrace of houses, follow the flight of steps right, down to the harbour wall and turn left along the road (not the private drive) towards the pier. At the pier, either take a detour to the lighthouse, or keep left before the cottages, along a walled lane around the headland.

The present pier was built between 1810 and 1821 to replace previous efforts in the 13th and 16th centuries. The sheltered waters of the river mouth have been adopted by a famous flock of mute swans; the numbers have ebbed and flowed over the years according to breeding success and pollution, but there are always a few about, even in the middle of summer. Long life and loyalty (to home and mate) are essential features of swan ecology.

The Tweed is renowned for its salmon fishing, with many anglers regarding it as the best in the UK. In centuries past, most salmon were caught near the mouth of the river using 'sweep nets' which were cast from small boats or cobles. This was a vital industry for Berwick and the neighbouring community of Spittal on the south side of the estuary, providing food, employment and an important source of income. Whilst this type of fishing has all but died out, angling is big business with some of the best 'beats' now costing as much as £4000 per rod per week and the salmon being caught on 'flies' that go by such colourful names as Hairy Mary and Munro Killer.

As the road takes a left turn to a small car park, bear right along the cliff-top path beside the golf course.

The open ground between the town and the sea, now a golf course, was once occupied by a leper hospital and is still called the Magdalen Fields. The rigg and furrow marks of mediaeval ploughing are still visible, though any cultivation here probably finished by the time the ramparts were built. In later centuries, and as recently as the 1940s, cattle grazed the Magdalen Fields and were driven each night through the Cow Port.

About 200 metres past the Coastguard Station, take the tarmac path heading left along the top of a ridge running back towards the town walls.

This path follows a ridge just south of the 'Covered Way', a broad deep trench running from below Brass Bastion to the cliff-top. It was excavated in 1565 as an obstacle to enemies and a safe path to a cliff-top fort.

There are good views northwards, to the two old cliff-side quarries which provided most of the stone for the building of the ramparts.

Cross the road on the far side of the golf course, turn right along the tarmac path and take the first left turn beside Brass Bastion. Walk along the base of the ramparts past Cumberland Bastion back to the car park.

The low ground in front of the ramparts was once a water-filled ditch. The water was shallow until half way across, where there was a sudden twelve foot trench. Whole armies could have drowned having a secret paddle.